spectacular
POOLS

WATSON
GUPTILL

AUTHOR

Francisco Asensio Cerver

EDITORIAL MANAGER

Jordi Vigué

PROJECT CO-ORDINATOR

Ivan Bercedo / Itziar Sen

DESIGN AND LAYOUT

Mireia Casanovas Soley

TEXT

Ivan Bercedo / Itziar Sen

TRANSLATION

Harry Paul

COPY EDITING

Michael Webb

PHOTOGRAPHY

Pere Planells
Eugeni Pons (On a Greek Islands)

1999 © FRANCISCO ASENSIO CERVER

ISBN

0-8230-6633-9

DLB

11.480-99

PRINTED IN SPAIN

Gràfiques Ibèria s.a.

First published in 1999 by arco for Hearst Books International

1350 Avenue of the Americas

New York, NY 10019

Distributed in the U.S. and Canada by

Watson-Guptill Publications

1515 Broadway

New York, NY 10036

Distributed throughout the rest of the world by

Hearst Books International

1350 Avenue of the Americas

New York, NY 10019

Few constructions better illustrate the culture of leisure and comfort than the swimming pool. Although on some occasions it can play a religious, landscapist, or sporting role, the image of a swimming pool is almost always associated with lazy hours enjoyed in a bathing suit in the intense sun—the only concern being to finish your cocktail before the ice cubes melt.

Adding a swimming pool to a private house certainly increases the quality of life, not only because of its intrinsic advantages but also because it suggests a benign climate and an idyllic life in the open air. A swimming pool is obviously a privilege that depends on geography. With the exceptions of a few brave enthusiasts who use a pool in the winter in Germany, Illinois, or Scotland, in general a swimming pool is associated with Mediterranean countries, with California, or Australia—that is, regions that enjoy a mild climate, typically with a variety of holiday resorts nearby.

The proliferation of pools has taken place near the coast and not inland, a fact which demonstrates that the pool is not meant as a substitute for the sea, but rather as a refinement of existing beach culture.

Swimming pools located next to the sea are common, and this book explores several examples. Some even have both the natural and artificial surfaces of water superimposed visually upon each other.

Until not long ago private swimming pools were exclusively for the affluent. However, the second half of the twentieth century saw a steady decline in the relative prices of pool construction, while during the same period the purchasing power of the middle class steadily rose. As a result, broad sections of society now enjoy the luxury of a private pool. Building a swimming pool today is often more a matter of deciding how best to enhance the urban landscape than how to meet costs.

In the following pages we have not set out to do a swimming pool construction manual, nor even a catalogue of models. What we have tried to show is the extraordinary richness and diversity of an architectural element that has deep historical roots and that in recent years has experienced impressive evolution and development.

We have not chosen the pools based on their size, cost, or location, but rather for their originality as solutions to problems posed by their particular situation. In every case the construction of the pool was decided with a clear goal in mind, such as to achieve a special landscaping appearance or to recreate certain aesthetics, either by imaginatively transforming the surroundings or by integrating the man-made elements into the natural scenery.

With these considerations in mind, the book has been divided into four chapters, with each covering a particular theme: Nature, The Historical Inheritance, Water in Architecture, and Pure Geometry. These chapters do not try to back up any thesis or doctrine, nor do they aim to favor any particular style compared to another. They simply group together different types of pools according to their design approach.

Nature

The most ancient predecessors of the swimming pool were lakes or the still waters of a river. These have always been places chosen by swimmers for amusement and relaxation. Today, many urban people dream of taking a dip in a tranquil pond or brook, far away from the noise and the bustle of the city. For that reason, swimming pool designers often try to recreate a natural look. In this chapter we have included swimming pools that enhance and fit comfortably into their natural surroundings. Many mechanisms can be used to emphasize the symbiosis between vegetation and water, such as irregular perimeters, artificial islands or water falls, or natural beaches with rocks marking off the edges.

According to its designer, Rolph Blakstad, the shape of this swimming pool is directly inspired by its location. The pool is sited on a small meseta which ends abrubtly in cliffs running down to the sea. Facing west, the pool is ideally located to catch the last rays of the evening sun and to enjoy the glorious sight of the sun setting over the ocean.

This is not a grandiose pool—the dimensions are about 26 feet by 54 feet, with a depth of only 4 feet. It is irregularly shaped, with a small area of sand and a cascade that was built to take advantage of the precipitous drop. The falling water of the cascade is a visual link between the pool and the sea. At sunset they are bathed in a rich golden color in which their waters seem to melt together.

On the cliff top itself, a small classically styled pavilion has been built, a simple rectangular gazebo with wooden beams supported by four groups of three Doric columns placed in a straight line at each corner. From the gazebo there are wide-ranging views over the pool and the sea, making it the perfect sort of place for whiling away a lazy afternoon or dining al fresco during the summer months. On the other edge of the cliff top, Rolph Blaksted has built a brick bench oriented toward the swimming pool.

These two new constructions frame the cascade which lies between them. An extra surprise lies hidden by the nearby trees—a wooden construction, reached by a stairway of the same material, which is both romantic and playful. Like a tree house, it offers possibilities for children's games and lover's trysts.

One of the main attractions of this pool is its orientation and its integration with the landscape. Its perimeter forms a type of bay that culminates in a cascade connecting the pool visually with the sea. The pool faces west, so that in the evening one can swim in the light of the setting sun.

*The gazebo has wonderful
views over the sea and is an
ideal site for picnics or
dinners in the open air.*

*The pool is surrounded by a
pine copse. A contrasting line
of palm trees has been
planted around the pool itself.*

A small wooden
playhouse has been built
among the branches of
the surrounding pines.

The pool is surrounded by a ring of flagstones, which gives way to a large expanse of grass. The cascade is framed by two asymmetrical constructions; a long bench and a wooden gazebo.

Of all the pools presented in this book, perhaps the furthest-removed from the conventional idea of the rectangular swimming pool is the pool shown here, with its natural perimeter that looks as if it has been designed by chance. Located at the foot of a rocky mountain bare of vegetation, its designers gave full expression to their sense of empathy with the surroundings. They designed a swimming pool that seems almost like a lake or natural pool.

This empathy with the place takes the form of a dialogue between the shapes that surround the surface of the water in the foreground and the abrupt mass of the mountain providing the backdrop— a recurring theme throughout the design. Nearly the entire border of the pool is constructed of local, irregularly placed rocks. As a result, the water has no defined continuous limits and the perimeter is constantly broken, forming tiny areas where aquatic vegetation grows. Some of the rocks are actually still in their original sites and rise from the original surface level of the ground.

Remarkably, the construction of the pool has involved barely any modification of the former landscape. Instead, the new construction has been integrated into the terrain while becoming immersed in it.

On one side of the pool, a small terrace with regular paving extends out in a fan shape. This artificial area in the middle of the natural landscape is the center of social activity and is equipped with a sunshade and easy chairs, as well as a set of steps allowing easy access to the pool.

The surrounding garden contains a few pieces of modern sculpture together with restored traditional constructions such as a stone irrigation channel. This philosophy of accepting the site as it existed beforehand and not trying to modify it is the reflection of a respectful attempt to establish a dialogue with the landscape—an attitude that also reflects the lifestyles of those using this idyllic place. Perhaps the image which sums this philosophy up best is that of a hammock hanging lazily between two trees.

A nearly vertical, rocky mountainside rises behind the pool and its silhouette is an ever-present force looming above the garden.

The owners have incorporated local, vernacular elements, both in the layout of the garden and in the furniture.

Without a doubt, the best way to spend the hot mid-summer afternoons is to recline under the shade of a spreading tree.

NO LIMITS

People living in hot climates spend a lot of time in the open air, and usually seek the protection of their homes only during occasional bouts of bad weather or when they feel the need for more intimacy. Hot coastal areas often have a common architecture that is a response to the climatic conditions characteristic of these zones—intense sunlight, a high level of humidity, refreshing coastal breezes and high temperatures nearly all year.

This architecture often includes roofs with eaves or cantilevered balconies and verandas which create shade and protect doors and windows from direct sunlight. Blinds and brise-soleils filter the light, while allowing as much to penetrate as is comfortable. The façades of coastal dwellings are considerably enriched by these additions, which permit sunlight and heat to be controlled according to the season.

When so much time is spent outdoors, the swimming pool naturally becomes the focus of social and physical activity. Therefore, the pool site should be carefully chosen, taking into account not only the preferences of the owner,

Although there is a predominance of straight lines and rigid divisions, the house ihas not been given over to sterile symmetry. The shapes are full of dynamism and vitality.

but also a series of other factors such as orientation, hours of sunlight, presence of trees nearby, and views.

In the case of the pool featured here, the location is due mainly to the fantastic views over the sea provided in a treeless area defined only by a low hedge marking the beginning of a gentle slope down to the rocks. The curved shape of the pool adapts snugly and sinuously to the profile of the land, and is finished by a surrounding of porous, anti-slip, rustic quarry tiles. The same tiles are used to pave the terraces surrounding the house.

The surface of the water lends added beauty to the garden, and can be seen from the living rooms of the house. The brick and stone walls reach beyond the house to divide the exterior and lead down to the pool. The curves of the landscape suggest a feeling of movement and contrast with the straight lines of the architecture.

Common natural materials were used in an attempt to unify the site and the architectural design, diluting the division between interior and exterior. The windows are aligned so as to give maximum control of daylight in the main rooms of the house. Some of the windows are framed by the verandas or balconies.

Although the final objective of a pool is to swim in it, water offers many possibilities which should not be forgotten about if you want to enrich the landscape. In this book we contemplate a wide range of projects in which the swimming pool has become an important focal point in the garden.

Constructing a swimming pool enables us to introduce into the garden some especially attractive natural water scenes: a beach, a river, a still pond or a lake. Among all of them, perhaps the most enchanting is a waterfall. Is there anyone who has not wanted to dive into the water beneath a waterfall in the midst of nature's beauty. It is beyond doubt that the owners of this swimming pool are admirers of these natural retreats. Building a swimming pool in their garden presented them with the opportunity to simultaneously add a waterfall. They took advantage of it.

Of course, this has been possible thanks to the different levels that already existed in the garden, but also thanks to the intelligent way in which they got the most out of the topography, and the great care they dedicated to each zone. Indeed, constructing a swimming pool was part of a general ordering of all the garden spaces. The land has been divided up into relaxation areas, places where thick vegetation grows, paths, stairs and terraces.

The swimming pool is relatively small. Starting from the waterfall, the pool spreads out in an irregular shape into the garden. Its edges are softly curved, just like the pools that nature has formed at the foot of wild falls. After the first fall the water drops further into another small pond at a lower level.

Around the pool grassy areas have been combined with a specially preserved wood pavement.

A circuit of paths and stairs allows you to make a lap around the pool edge and to come back to where the waterfall starts.

A curved concrete wall separates the swimming pool from a small pond on a lower level.

Around the pool leisure areas are side by side with thick vegetation. The astute way in which they have been worked together produces a highly realistic natural look.

BLENDING WITH THE LANDSCAPE

In the middle of an orange grove, which seems to contain every possible shade of green, the transparent blue color of this pool stands out. However, the plane of water is not isolated from the landscape; instead it has been integrated by treating the pool not as a static object but rather by looking at the water as a liquid element and using this to create a natural path. There are few things more naturally harmonious in nature than that a river that struggles to be born, from the first springs emerging from the rocks to the way the infant river fights the land to gain its own territory. This design reproduces a fragment of this struggle, incorporating nature's tempo, the cadence of flowing water with its relaxing sounds. The large boulders uncovered by excavation work have been arranged to form a river bed which leads right up to the pool itself.

The design, both of the house and the pool, takes the presence of the orange grove as its starting point. The compositional force of the fields, demonstrating the work of man in harmony with nature, the special order of the trees and the terraces with their protecting stone walls are elements which the architects and owners have used as guidelines for this new work.

The result is a design which perfectly combines the rational with the natural and seeks to establish a mutually beneficial dialogue with the landscape.

As a finishing touch, one side of the pool is protected by an open space flanked by arcades washed in an earthy red tone.

The watercourse, with its
eddies and tiny cascades
create dynamic visual
forces that contrast with
the stillness of the pool.

The presence of the orange
groves is the starting point of
the design of both the house
and the pool.

Placed to benefit from the best
views of the landscape, this
small veranda offers some
shade to protect from the
summer sunshine.

There are a series of images that are immediately associated with a country house: being near nature, beholding the landscape every morning, or wanting to adapt to a less stressful life style. Most of the population carry out their daily activities in a city context, characterised by the square shapes and the hectic velocity of life.

Anybody who decides to build a house in the country or in the mountains, or to refurbish an already existing one, has to take on board a consequence of their initial decision: they have decided to live in a certain degree of isolation, be more tranquil, move closer to the simpler things in life, and shed off the obligations and restraints of having their residence in the city.

This is a typical rural house which takes advantage of the mountain slope. On one of the terraces a swimming pool is situated. The architecture goes beyond the outside walls: its lines, surfaces and volumes incorporate the garden into the home. The spaces can be admired as you walk around, for if we stand still we cannot take in all its beauty. The vegetation complements the construction work, creating shady zones where we can rest from the merciless summer sun.

The water is in contact with one of the containment walls of the ground and of the house. This reinforces the integration effect: the different volumes that make up the residence have been used as architectural elements that enhance the pool. The colors of the materials form a varied palette. Every feature is an individual brushstroke, a careful detail, that subtly changes the texture and marries the stone with the greenery.

The different levels mean that the
swimming pool can be come
upon from surprising view points.

ON A GREEK ISLAND

The capitals spread around the site, the masonry walls, and the beheaded statues cut out against the horizon lead us to guess the location of this pool: the island of Corfu in the Adriatic sea. The vegetation in the garden is made up of species that are typical in this part of the world: olives, cypresses and aromatic plants. Not only do all of them integrate the pool into the environment, but they also complete the ancient mythical Greece look of the landscape.

The most outstanding characteristic of the swimming pool, however, is its magnificent location. A flat terrace halfway up a white cliff offers a spectacular view over the bay, and at the same time protects from the wind.

The way the pool is designed fosters this dual relationship with the sea and the rocks. The cliff face runs down to the water surface, and the opposite edge of the swimming pool stretches away to the infinity: a hardly visible line against the background of the sea and the sky.

The cliff has imposed on the pool an irregular geometric form, although the two ends are defined and straight edged. One side has been paved with indigenous stone, extracted from the lowered cliff which has been used as a quarry. At the foot of one of the vertical faces, next to the swimming pool, a deep red colored canvas canopy has been set up.

At the other end some little steps lead up to the house where an ample porch welcomes the visitor. It is an intermediate space between the outside and the inside. The gable roof is of Arabic tiles on top of a wood truss structure. Behind the porch, which provides the shade, the façade of the house is formed by a series of seven stilted arches. Curiously behind these arcades a second pool has been constructed; it is square and smaller. However, it is not a redundant element for it is radically different to the outside swimming pool. It is a counterweight and contrast: compared to the open design and landscapist vocation of the outside pool, this second one has an intimate character. It is closely linked to the architectural language of the house.

From the swimming pool, a
Mediterranean garden descends
until the limit of the cliff.

The night view of the swimming
pool makes the most of the
dramatism of the rock. To
accentuate the effect the lighting
system is projected upwards.

A view of the inside pool
surrounded by arcades.

One of the most interesting aspects of the garden is the high quality of the pavement stones. The color differences between the slabs give the floor an enormous visual richness.

Classical Greece is evoked explicitly by the capitals and the statues, and also implicitly by using plants and materials typical of the Hellenic gardens.

THE HISTORICAL INHERITANCE

Another reference, just as important as nature, is history. Swimming pools, ponds, and fountains have been indispensable elements in the architecture of many civilizations. Landscape architecture and the design of private pools and gardens are full of features inspired by roman villas, Arabian style patios, renaissance or baroque palaces, or far eastern edifices. In this chapter we have included swimming pools that have used this inheritance as a design source. This chapter features Arabian inspired pavilions, neoclassical fountains, pergolas with classical columns and porticos.

In the succession between the spaces in western architecture there is an immaterial axis which is like an arrow flying toward the vanishing point. In oriental

architecture the style goes along a similar path. This axis joins together the spaces. Firstly, because axis implies continuity. And secondly because it represents focus and a unique orientation and perspective. Continuity becomes discontinuity and focalisation does not exist. A unique direction turns into a multiple one; a straight line breaks up and curves. In oriental architecture one goes from one space to another with no other architectural rhythm than the dazzle of the light and the contrasting shade. The special interest in open spaces, patios, yards, quadrangles and gardens is also characteristic of this culture.

In this project an effort has been made to follow these premises when organizing the space around the pool. An oriental style has been used and can be noticed in the small pavilion on one side of the pool with its series of arches, the woodwork and the marble columns.

The water zones have been carefully thought out. They are the focus of an Islamic style garden. The theme evoked is the meeting of four rivers in paradise. This cosmic cross has been achieved by placing two small square ponds full of lotuses. The functional and aesthetic elements have been combined to create a geometric tapestry of different textures. The bathing zone occupies a central rectangle. Everything adds up to form a palette of diverse colors that go through the blue and green range framed by the ochre tone of the stone. The proportions of each element were not left to chance: they were calculated together in accordance with the symbolic geometry.

Next to the swimming pool there are geometric parterres with grass or little ponds brimming with lotus flowers.

This garden of this open space is well cared for. It includes tree and vegetation species from the region: palm trees, fruit trees, scented plants and creepers among others.

The white of the small pavilions stands out against the green and blue tones of the garden.

At one end there is a
small pavilion decorated
in an oriental style. It
combines materials like
wood and marble.

A MOORISH POOL

Water is unquestionably the center of this garden, which tries to synthesize the Arab and Greco-Roman traditions within a main theme—the four rivers of Paradise. The swimming pool itself is a rectangle whose sides have a 3:1 proportion. This is complemented by a lotus pond which represents the Cosmic Cross and whose measurements are a Pythagorean 3:4:5. The measurements of both bodies of water are in cubits (the Phoenician unit of measurement often mentioned in the Bible). Thus, while the main pool measures 8 by 24 cubits, the smaller one is 6 by 8.

The measurements of the pavilions at the ends and sides of the pools, and the siting of the trees, are harmoniously linked by proportions measured in cubits and based on studies made of the gardens of Shalimar in Kashmir and of the ancient gardens of Iraq. The plants chosen represent those used in medieval Arab gardens and include a wide selection of Damascus roses.

The style of the pavilions varies, with some being straight imitations of Arab architecture and others reinterpretations of this tradition with touches that allude to the Roman world. At one end of the site there is a small pavilion with pointed arches and elaborate plasterwork the borders of which seem to lead off into infinity. The roof is pyramidal and is constructed of green enameled tiles—a sacred color in Islam. At the opposite end of the site, a fountain, formed by a

vaulted niche crowned by an arch bearing a classical pediment, introduces the language of Western culture into the garden.

The resulting fusion of different traditions is based on the use of geometrical laws. The axes, symmetries, and proportions associated with exact mathematical formulas are revealed as the repositories of secret, metaphysical laws which carry an eternal message.

It is, of course, evident that this is a swimming pool in name only, not to be used for bathing, but rather to be appreciated with the mind and the senses.

The pavilions are surrounded by exuberant vegetation.

Green tiled roofs are sacred
elementin some Islamic
countries.

White is the dominant color of
all the pavilions.

Every'thing in the garden
is associated with a
precise symbology and no
element is unplanned.

Following Arab traditions, the
garden is an enclosed world,
and represents a universe both
metaphorical and domestic.

*The water is never
still, but gushes from
fountains and sprinklers.*

Although Lady Latymer is not exactly a lover of swimming pools, persistent urging by younger members of her family led her to have one built at her summer villa in Majorca next to the water tank in the garden that she herself had designed some three years earlier. Lady Latymer paid

special attention to two things: first, the integration of the pool with the garden and the style of the house, and second, the safety of the pool.

A small pavilion with a veranda, a tiny kitchen, a bath, and a shower was built to complement the pool. Judy Latymer admits that she "wanted to give it a slightly oriental, tropical look; not like some delicately filigreed Arab building, but something weightier which was more in tune with the architecture of the house."

The balustrade which crowns the pavilion is a copy of one which can be found in one of the corners of the garden, together with some nineteenth-century statuary, all acquired by the first owners of the property. Opposite the pavilion, on the other side of the pool, is a flight of steps that descends through two clumps of trees and continues on into the pool itself. The broad terracotta steps also serve as impromptu seating. The paths and borders of the pool are built from a mixture of cement, sand, and local earth, giving them a warm color.

"One of my daughters broke her nose jumping into a shallow pool, so I insisted that ours should be 10 feet deep all over. If someone can't swim, they'll have to wear a float or sit and watch," adds Lady Latymer.

This concern for safety also extends to the household animals. Judy Latymer decided to build a parapet around the pool so that none of the animals could accidentally fall in and drown.

The design allows the more adventurous to dive into the pool from the parapet, while the less exuberant can descend calmly using the stairway.

Lady Latymer wanted to give the pool the look of an old, open-air water deposit, so that it would merge smoothly with the garden and the overall aesthetic of the house. To achieve this, the pool is not finished with the blue mosaic tiling, but instead is given a fresh coat of white paint every year.

The sculptures date from the last century, when the villa was enlarged and refurbished

A copper filter is used to keep the pool clean, as members of the family do not like swimming in chlorinated water.

The flat surface of the
swimming pool reflects the
lodge and complements it.
Protected by the shadow of
the building, one can recline
on the chairs like a Roman
senator and contemplate the
surrounding fields.

This garden is architectural. It could be a village square except that the swimming pool makes us think it is a private space. The elements are marked out by white rims that isolate them and bestow upon them a certain sculpuresque quality.

The strict form of the swimming pool, with its right angles, reinforces the hard geometry of the architecture and the wall. A solid, sturdy and static air impregnates the ambience. It is a space that the light orders. In the entrance zone of the house there is an arcade style porch, under the arches of which the darkness contrasts with the white façade. A wall pergola runs around the patio framing the views over the palm tree-dotted slope. They even go as far as taking over an isolated area of the garden.

This form of landscapism reminds us of the sculptures realised by the land art artists. These lonely sculptures situated on the virgin high plateaus of South America give the sites their uniqueness. The placing of these monuments was the start of the project idea.

The sensation that the site puts over is as important as the direct information we obtain from it. Landscape architecture includes all the space outside the lines of the building. It is not just parks, gardens and squares, but rather any space that is in the open air.

The entrance is a shady
zone that acts as a
transition space
between the soft light
inside and the blinding
sun in the garden.

This small gardened plaza is a view point over the hillslope, a balcony looking out onto the landscape.

The swimming pool container
juts out of the ground slightly,
making a very useful rim.

Space and volume are two sides of the same architectural coin. There is a way of designing from the inside to the outside without regard for the outward appearance of the design.

The resulting design, however, is not merely a product of chance but rather the pure exterior expression of the interior. If the terrain has a pronounced gradient, the most rational and economic solution is to adapt to the land by creating terraces, and this is the solution adopted by the designer shown here.

The pool adopts organic shapes and faithfully follows the contour line created by the terracing until it approaches the edge, when this natural harmony is broken by a rigid, completely abstract straight line—so straight that the water seems as though it has been cut by a knife. Two cypress trees rise from the terrace below like two thin, vertical lines which contrast with the horizontal plane of the water.

The pool is reached by a stone stairway that opens out onto an area with reclining chairs of a contemporary design. However, for those who are impatient to reach the water, the stairs branch off to arrive directly at the pool, just where another flight of steps leads down into the water.

A good way to ensure harmony with the landscape is to pause and look around to see what materials are native to the landscape and then to use them whenever possible. In this way, the colors and textures of the new materials blend in with the surroundings.

The style of furniture is also important. The overall look of the design can be greatly influenced by the type of chairs and tables that are chosen.

The beauty of this pool lies in large part with the contrast between the organic shape and the straight line imposed as the pool approaches the edge of the terrace.

The architectural elements are perfectly adapted to the terrain, and the result is a design that is in harmony with the landscape.

Some wooden easy chairs placed at one end of the pool are ideal for relaxed sunbathing.

During Roman times, one of the main social centers was the public baths, known as thermae. Evidence for this comes from the fact that the famous Thermae of Caracalla were, together with the Coliseum and the Hippodrome, one of the largest buildings constructed in Rome itself. Although the baths are often seen as a social meeting place for the public, their main functions were more prosaic ones such as bathing, grooming, and relaxation. The importance of bathing is further underlined by the fact that the villas of the rich always possessed their own private baths. The pool shown here attempts to recapture the tradition of the Roman baths.

This indoor pool fills nearly an entire room, and is unusually long and narrow—in fact, its width is less than 10 feet, the minimum space necessary for one person to swim comfortably with arms extended. Its depth is minimal, as is the space surrounding it. The ceiling is supported by wooden beams. The simplicity of the room is alleviated by a Roman bust placed on a marble pedestal, a bench, and two plants filling the corners of the space.

Daylight enters by means of a small, square window situated just above the bench and by a small side window. The lighting is deliberately tenuous. Light is reflected on the walls painted in an earthy color and again on the surface of the water. The whole atmosphere of the pool is one of relaxation and serenity—a feeling accentuated at night, when the room is lit by candles.

The links with Roman culture are highlighted by some of the small decorative details. On one of the side walls a portico has been painted, formed by a line of Ionic columns joined by a series of lowered arches, while the bottom of the swimming pool is enlivened by a rectangular border which, seen through the water, suggests a Roman mosaic.

The decorative details of the pool room are full of references to the Classical world.

This small, indoor swimming pool, with its Roman atmosphere, is not merely private but also intensely intimate. Its dimensions make it difficult to imagine more than two people bathing at once.

WATER IN ARCHITECTURE

Swimming pools are normally located in outdoor gardens but there are alluring examples which break this general rule. In fact, the Roman spas and Turkish baths were built inside. Furthermore, even outdoor pools can be more closely linked to nearby buildings than to the landscape or vegetation. In this chapter we present swimming pools that have a close relationship with the nearby architecture.

The architectural intervention that has made this swimming pool possible can be described as a surgical operation. Because the swimming pool is at a partial-basement level, the problem of relating it with the garden and the living room had to be resolved with a kind of spatial pirouette. The natural meeting point between the house and the garden has been dug so that a semicircular

staircase could be built. This staircase leads to the partial-basement level.

The staircase has been conceived as a continuation of the garden. The steps are constructed out of ceramic bricks with soil between them so that vegetation can grow. A ramp leads to the living room, stopping just before the staircase. A glass and aluminum structure defines the division between garden and swimming pool. A folding, sliding door allows the pool to be opened up completely to the garden or closed off in case of harsher weather. The roof is made of acid-etched glass and therefore provides a direct visual link between the living room and swimming pool.

The swimming pool is a perfect circle. One half is a step higher than the other. Both the inside of the pool and the walls of the room are covered by a mosaic, while the floor is made of a tropical wood parquet that is resistent to humidity. Around the entire edge of the pool the parquet has been finished off with a simple stainless steel rim.

The swimming pool water jet is incorporated into a fountain located just below the wooden ramp. A channel carries the water from the fountain to the swimming pool. The ramp is supported by a stainless steel pillar.

The swimming pool's
location in the partial
basement made it possible
to conserve all of the
existing small garden.

Dividing the wooden platforms around the pool into quadrants gave the designers the chance to make patterns out of the parquet strips.

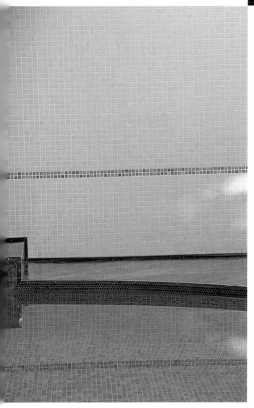

Both this house and its swimming pool are in an unparalleled location. Built into the side of one of the hills that surround Barcelona, the pool has an uninterrupted panoramic view of almost 180 degrees over the city and the Mediterranean.

Although this location is undoubtedly privileged, it also meant that the design was heavily conditioned by a single fact. The gradient of the hill at this point is nearly 40 percent, and so a series of containing walls were needed to form terraces on different levels, which now contain the garden and the pool.

In fact, the pool was constructed not by sinking it into the ground, but as a hanging structure supported by pillars, girders, and a concrete slab—filled out with gravel in order to adjust to the gradient. A layer of Gunite forms a second, interior skin.

The pool is not enclosed. Therefore, it affords visual continuity with the horizon. The sea, almost 16 kilometers away, seems quite close and is integrated visually into the garden.

Surrounding the pool the architects have built a platform of teak. The house is a few meters away from the pool and is aligned with it. The main façade has a flat, glass face, protected by a teak marquee, which is supported by two-story-high, round metal pillars. The marquee works on two scales; house and garden. Its style converts it into the element that unites both.

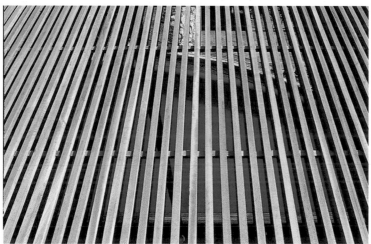

The architects chose to use a bright blue mosaic in the pool, which contrasts with the dark tone of the teak wood. The borders of the pool are also built from teak, which is famous for its water-resistent properties.

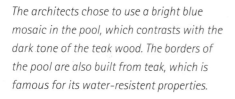

The extremely thin metal pillars gives the marquee an extraordinary lightness.

When seen from the house, the vertical succession of terraces in the garden appears as a series of colored parallel strips, interspersing the colors of the burnt earth, the green grass, the blue pool, and the brown wood.

This swimming pool has been built in the inner garden of an old town villa with masonry walls and wide stone arches. The pool provides a fine example of how to integrate a new element into a space that has already been consolidated. The relationship between the house, the shared walls, and the swimming pool has been designed in such a natural way that nobody would imagine that these elements were built in different periods.

Although the materials used have a vernacular look, and the general image is one of traditional architecture. The complex composition of different planes at distinct levels seems to be inspired by neoplastic compositions.

The surroundings of the pool are heterogeneous. The architects have designed spaces on both sides of the pool which have different characteristics: a flat grass lawn, a porch with a tiled roof, an elevated platform that runs into a stone wall going around the pool, and a series of terraces, stairs, and arches linking the garden to the house. Therefore, although the swimming pool is practically rectangular it has a multifaceted character which takes it away from the habitual uniformity of many pools of this type. In this case the unique appearance has been achieved by playing with the heights, the materials, and the way the sun falls on each zone.

The garden design is not based exclusively on either functional or aesthetic questions—technical factors have also been considered. In this respect, the water jet embedded in the side wall of the pool is not merely one of the most visually eye-catching elements in the garden, it is also one of the pieces that give the garden its overall form. The substantial width of the jet means that a massive flow of high-pressure water can come out.

To make this possible the interior reservoir needed a capacity fifty per cent as great as that of the swimming pool. This meant that the height of the side platform had to be determined by the dimensions of the underground reservoir.

The shared walls separating the garden from the neighboring houses are quite high. However, the breadth of the space has meant that this can be turned into an advantage.
The creeper plants clinging to the wall are an additional point of interest in the garden.

The constant gushing of water from the jet is one of the most lively elements in the garden.

A vaulted tunnel leads from the house entrance to the swimming pool.

A series of terraces on different levels, which receive the sunlight to varying degrees, surround the pool.

This pool was built as part of a larger project of remodeling an old house in the country. Although the conversion did not involve any major changes in the architecture or external appearance of the house, the surrounding land has been radically altered. What was once farmland has been transformed into landscaped grounds, with a large expanse of well-tended lawn and a careful selection of decorative plants. A small pool was built to complete this transformation.

The most important and decisive aspect of the pool is its siting. Instead of the conventional placement in the center of a garden surrounded by lawns, the designers have chosen to build it in an irregular corner, so that the rough masonry walls of the house loom directly above it.

As a result of this unusual location, the pool is more or less L-shaped, with one of the sections penetrating the walls

and running under a buttress-shaped stone arch. The other section of the pool is separated from the garden by a small stone wall about 3 feet high, which is decorated with potted plants. The other side of this small dividing wall has been paved with terracotta flagstones to form a terrace where various reclining chairs and benches have been placed.

This layout means that access to the pool is in practice limited to one of its narrowest sides, where offset stairs allow easy access to the water. The walls of the pool are dressed with mosaics of an intense blue, which contrasts strongly with the surrounding stone walls.

Because of its size and location, this is not really a pool for swimming. It should be seen as a place to relax and capture the freshness of the water, especially in summer. In some ways it brings to mind the water cisterns of old farmhouses, and can even be seen as a miniature version of the moats surrounding medieval castles.

The design of the garden balances the strong impression caused by the house and gives new meaning to some old, scattered outbuildings.

An impressive palm tree overshadows the pool.

An old storehouse was
demolished during the
conversion, leaving a space
to be occupied by the
swimming pool.

BETWEEN TWO WATERS

Like a Janus mask, with one face delighted and the other sullen, or one terrified and the other horrifying, this pool has two distinct and contrasting faces. The bather who enters the pool on one side encounters a rectangular pool of traditional construction, while on the other side the pool becomes curved and irregular, conforming more to the laws of nature than to those of man.

This duality is not just visual. It also serves both as a functional division and as an extension of the architectural laws that define the dwelling and garden which the pool serves. Thus, the rectangular portion of the pool is deeper and ideal for serious swimming, while on the other side, the small meandering inlets, the shallow areas, and the smoothly descending stairs are designed for more relaxed and leisurely enjoyment.

The rectangular part of the pool has a more direct relationship with the house, as the paved area around it connects directly with the porch and entrance to the

pavilion. At the same time, the opposite half of the pool is linked to the garden and lawn that extend from the pool's edge to the nearby pine copse. In fact, the pool seems to be an inlet that forms a small peninsula intruding into the garden. At its furthest reach, a palm tree has been planted as an echo of the nearby woods.

The pavilion, which complements the pool, was built after the pool. The structure is formed of thick pillars, beams, and trusses of wood supporting a sloped roof with an interior ceiling of tongue-and-groove boards and an exterior of Arab tiles.

The porch of the pavilion is large and roomy, and serves as an open-air lounge. A large wooden table dominates the space and is ideal for holding meals next to the pool or simply for playing cards, reading, or arguing about trivialities until the early hours. The interior of the pavilion consists of one large room closed off from the exterior by sliding glass doors.

The garden is nearly flat, which means that the principal views are dominated by the surrounding trees. The pool is the most important visual focus in the landscape. This small peninsula with its palm trees not only links the pool with the garden but also serves to provide a measure of privacy by partially hiding it from the veranda. The palm trees act as a natural divider.

The architects have used warm, natural materials throughout—the paving is terracotta, the roof is made of tiles, and wood is used for the structure and the window frames.

In this project a third element has been added to the typical house and swimming pool set up: a monumental staircase that goes down from the house to the pool. The slope of the land is so great that it became the most determinant architectural factor in the project. In fact, the staircase is more than twenty metres wide and has thirteen steps.

It is composed of a straight stretch, on top of which there is a round balcony, and a semi circular part. The inspiration from the drawings of Serlio, the Italian architect, is immediately evident.

What was vertical in the plans of the baroque theorist is horizontal here. Indeed, both the house and the garden are designed according to the Beaux Arts tradition. The architect of the house, Norman Cinamond, has established clear symmetrical axes which he has stuck to strictly.

However, despite this post modern vocation he preferred to use a modern language for the details. The result is a monumentalism so succinct that it recalls some of the projects of the German architect Albert Speer.

The swimming pool occupies one side of the garden. It runs from the center of the symmetry until the end of the site. One zone of the swimming pool is totally rectangle, while the other part has an irregular edge composed of varying curves.

There is a gangway which crosses both parts. The decision to make the two sections different was impulsed by the natural division between the two sides: on one side the garden commences, and on the other there is a straight lined, wood board terrace, in the vertex of which there is an bower.

This is a general view of the swimming
pool and the staircase. The façade of
the house is constructed out of white
brick. The staircase is artificial stone.
The teak wood bestows elegance on the
gangway, while at the bottom of the
pool there is a blue mosaic.

The staircase permits an interesting
view looking down on the pool.

The bower is a typical element in the Beaux Arts tradition. It is used to define a key point in the composition and to mark out some visual perspectives.

Although the main rooms of the house are on the upper floor, below the staircase a bathroom has been fitted out.

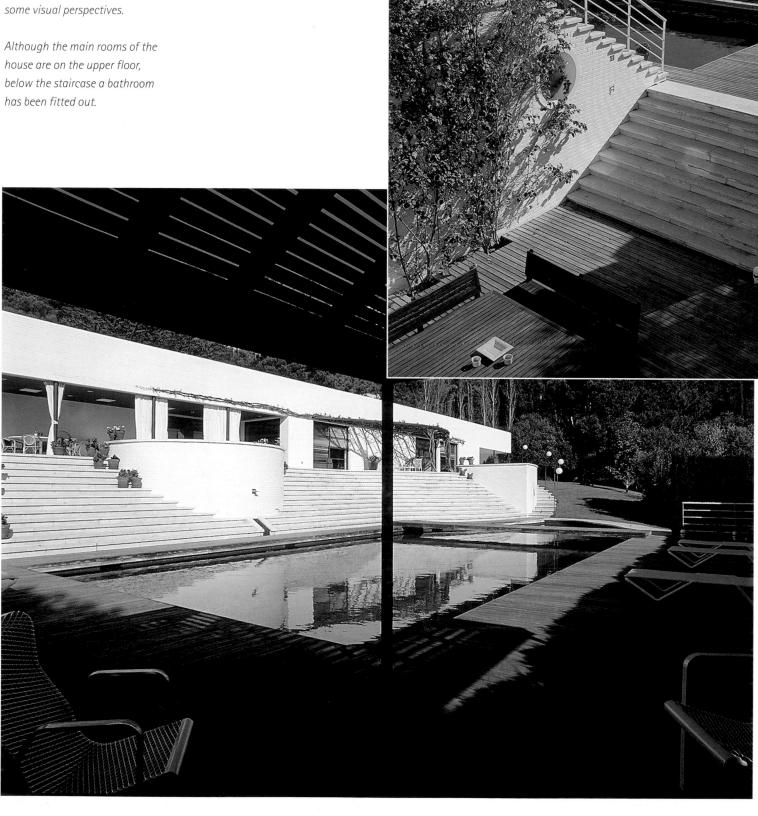

In order to use hillsides as cultivable land and to avoid the danger of earth-slides caused by excessive rain, artificial terraces, usually contained within stone walls, have been used from ancient times as a way of carving out flat land where none exists. The resulting characteristic landscape is marked by the neatness of the dry stone walls descending into the valley.

Situated precisely on the edge of one of these laboriously created plots of land, this pool uses the containing walls as its own, thus becoming completely integrated into the landscape. It is not coincidence that the views over the surroundings are magnificent.

The point where the water meets the edge is marked by an area paved an area paved with teak wood- in reality a huge section of the trunk of the tree, which is large enough for sunbathing . Hidden beneath this huge section of trunk, the overflow limits the maximum level of the water, skimming off impurities and collecting water for recirculation.

Two water spouts provide fresh water for the pool and evoke images of old irrigation channels, of water troughs where the cattle sated their thirst, even of the public washing places where our great-grandmothers spent so much time - images indelibly linked to the functional architecture of the rural world. This pool uses elements of traditional architecture and converts them to new uses related to leisure and relaxation. The spouts are used to recirculate the water, and bring a touch of sound to the silence that surrounds the pool.

Perhaps the dominating theme in this design is that of the fountain. The water system of the old garden, in all its simplicity, maintained. The irrigation channels, although their function has changed, are a living reminder of ancient Moorish traditions.

The dry-stone walls rise above the concrete structures holding back the water and the earth. They also conceal the wall at the edge of the terrace. They are topped by a layer of limestone mortar which introduces a disturbing touch of white into a landscape dominated by greens and ochre tones.

The edge of the swimming
pool is made out of one
trunk. This required a great
deal of effort as there were
no trees this size nearby.

Near to the pool there is a recreation area.

The table and benches are brick-built and whitewashed, and arranged to form an angle that makes for intimate and friendly conversation.

The garden has been designed to fit in with the house. The use of different levels and the creation of areas with their own personality enrich the overall design. The non-invasive architecture, using hedges, low walls, pavements and plants to define different environments, helps to develop a landscape in consonance with the house.

In the traditional country garden, water often played an important role. Water channels, for example, gave gardens an aesthetic touch based on Moorish concepts of beauty, in addition to simply irrigating the garden. Today, many of these water systems have been converted into swimming pools.

The Balearic Islands have inherited influences from many different cultures, and Balearic architecture has assimilated the construction methods of each wave of invaders while also conserving a certain flavor that is uniquely its own. In recent years, the gardens in this region, with their terraces and pools, have undergone a distinct change in style, involving the adaptation of the English landscape tradition to the climate and flora of the islands. Instead of grand avenues with descending stairs or the symmetry and classical tradition inspired by Italian Renaissance villas, the trend is to create spaces that are more intimate and enclosed, and which are less grand and more domestic in scale.

This has led to a new interest in the idea of the market-garden, a tradition handed down from medieval times, with the planting of fruit trees, vines, laurel, and cypress trees. Orange trees have a long tradition of serving as decorative elements, being associated with the cloisters of convents and cathedrals of the Gothic period, with royal gardens, and with the patios of important civic buildings.

A small stone path flanked by a string of orange trees leads to the pool, which fits into the terrain thanks to an artificially created terrace jutting out over the slope on one side. As can be seen in the photos, the pool can also be reached by means of a stairway, which emerges onto a balcony built on one side of the pool. The balcony acts as a backdrop, as an elevation for the pool, and also as a refuge for escaping from the heat without losing the view of the surrounding landscape.

The small veranda provides
a corner of shade for
protection from the
afternoon sun.

The pool is reached by way
of a stone path flanked by
fruit trees.

The traditional architectural
style of rural houses is mixed
with a more modern and
functional sensibility.

This garden contains small, intimate, isolated areas where one can find solitude and enjoy nature and the architecture.

PURE GEOMETRY

One of the most widely used inspirations for designing swimming pools are geometric patterns. Pure forms, axes, and symmetries allow the surface of the water to be defined, and the garden to be organized, according to abstract and harmonious guidelines. Although such geometrical abstractions are in a sense an artificial order, they are nevertheless quite capable of invoking a balanced serenity if handled skillfully. The influences of composition techniques from the Beaux Arts school, vanguardist asymmetrical forms, and the modern movement have all been used to make geometry the basis of the design of these swimming pools. However, geometry has not limited the architectural vocabulary. On the contrary, it has provided a unifying logical structure in a wide range of situations.

The house is located between two small bodies of water- a pond and a swimming pool. The single-storey building is very simple, almost naïf. Formed by a series of parallel modules with sharply sloping roofs which give it a saw-tooth silhouette, the façades painted in red, combined with a reduced number of windows give it a somewhat disturbing surrealistic look.

However, a second, more considered appraisal reveals that this feeling comes not just from the house itself, but also from the relationship existing between it and the garden and the water. The house always appears as the vanishing point of a perspective; as the element which completes a composed landscape or as a reflection in the water. Just like the small pavilions in Moorish gardens, the building functions as a guideline which brings order to the landscape, establishing symmetries, axes and visual interplay.

In spite of the lack of any direct stylistic references, when we look at this small house, what springs to mind are images of the Alhambra or Marrakech.

The generous size of the garden, with its almost imperceptible gradient, is a determining force. The visual interplay is based on the control exercised by the designer over the garden's horizon. Around the house, there are a series of small, closed-in spaces which are at the same time interconnected and form a succession of ordered planes. The pool is located in one of these spaces - a garden completely enclosed by vegetation which converts it into a separate, intimate area. This division into independent areas is reflective of a culture which sees the garden not as a natural landscape, but rather as the considered product of human thought.

The distribution of the different areas is a reflection of the interior of the house - there are the main gardens, such as the one containing the pool, which function as lounges, accompanied by more private corners. Once it is understood that it is the garden which marks the real limits of the "dwelling" the actual house itself appears as a solitary object.

Although the surrounding terrain is practically flat, the house itself is on slightly raised ground which facilitates the views from and of the dwelling.

A system of peripheral
drainage means the surface
of the water is at the same
level as the paving
surrounding the pool.

*A metallic pergola which
supports climbing plants has
been built by the side of the
house. In summer it is one of
the most appreciated corners
of the garden.*

Between the Olives

This pool is located in a former olive grove that has been transformed into a private garden. The new owners have tried to conserve the essence of its previous use by leaving the olive trees in place as well as by maintaining the terraces with their supporting walls of rough stonework. The difference is that the terraces are now grassed over, so that what was before dry farming land has become a garden that needs irrigation.

The nearly rectangular pool lies in the middle of one of the olive terraces. It is aligned to follow the containing walls of the terraces. One end of the pool extends out in a semicircle containing steps that allow easy access to the pool. This semicircle, somewhat smaller than the width of the pool, also marks a symmetrical axis that creates geometric order in the garden.

To one side, camouflaged by one of the original retaining walls, there is a service room which is reached through an arch. The rhythm of the pillars suggests a Classical construction, but at the same time, the climbing plants which ascend the columns and become intertwined in the beams evoke the romantic images found in Piranesi´s engravings. The solitary air of the pergola and its relationship with the surrounding nature give it a decadent and bucolic feeling.

Around the pergola some wooden benches are distributed, seemingly at random. The cushions lying around are redolent of indolent conversations taking place while sprawled on the grass.

What this garden brings to mind is the myth of Arcadia—the ideal Arcadia as imagined during the Renaissance, with the pastoral, rural life in an immaculate paradise where the days slowly turn in step to the rhythms of nature.

The grass and wooden benches occupy
this old olive grove, giving it a feel of
being somewhat unmanicured. In
contrast to the rigorous order of the olive
trees and the containing walls supporting
the terraces, the cushions lying around on
the grass give another, rather different
idea of what is natural.

The pool is dressed with white mosaic tiles, and a narrow strip of surrounding terracotta tiles separates it from the grass.

The architects of this swimming pool have used the surface of the water to define the limit between the landscape and the building. The house is set on a teak platform that continues into the garden, which has been cut away to make three sides of the straight-lined and precise swimming pool. The rest of the garden is a green carpet of grass. Contrasting with the straight lines on the side nearest the house, the opposite edge is gently curved.

Lying between the varnished tropical wood and the intense green of the neatly trimmed grass, the swimming pool water takes on an energetic blue tone. This effect is due to the dark hue of the mosaic that covers the interior walls of the pool. The architects knew that the high quality of the materials used would bring out the best in all the elements. While the forms are unpretentious and geometric, the textures and the surfaces give the project its style.

The façade of the house has been done with noble and expensive materials: travertine and wood panels. The same attention to quality has been used to give the garden its distinguished look. The garden furniture, deck chairs, and a white sun screen use the same wood as the platform.

Four special stainless steel elements contrast with the white and wood backgrounds: the water jet, the ladder, the waste paper basket, and the shower. The porch pillars are also of stainless steel.

Next to the swimming pool a small pavilion has been built; its roof nicely serves as a place for different types of flowers and plants. A path built out of refinished railroad ties leads from the pool to a garden, across a soft, artificial grass slope. A short distance away lies the racket ball court, which is also covered with marble travertine.

The swimming pool has two distinct geometric lines: straight and curved.

The roof of the pool-side pavilion has been planted with various types of flowers and plants.

The stainless steel water jet is one of the most striking elements of the garden.

The swimming pool walls have been covered with an energetic blue that contrasts strongly with the green of the grass and the full tropical wood color.

This swimming pool lies in the middle of a wooden platform set in a conifer forest. The steep slope of the land made construction difficult and quite costly. Extra effort had to be made to find a balance between the small size of the pool and the desire to create as attractive a spot as possible.

The residence has been organized into two distinct zones. On one side the bedrooms are housed in a solid-looking, brick-walled block, and on the other side the common spaces are found within a triangle piece overlooking the magnificent views in front of the dwelling.

The terrace has also been divided according to the same considerations as the house. In front of the living room is an area in which to relax on some deck chairs. The swimming pool is in front of the bedroom block. The terrace is made entirely of wood. The hand rail, which runs along the edge of the platform and allows room for a wooden bench parallel to the pool, is a light stainless steel structure supported by taut cables like guy ropes.

The concrete walls that were installed to contain the swimming pool also contain a weight-training and fitness room. A round window from the gym looks out into the bottom of the pool. This allows daylight to pass into the gym through the pool, and produces soothing reflections that shimmer on the wall and pavement.

The swimming pool is
lit up at night.

The swimming pool
can be seen from the
bath on the first floor.

Green gardens full of overhanging trees that have taken years to reach their full glory are the ideal way of protecting our privacy. Inside this type of place a model microclimate is created which is highly propitious for getting away from that fazed out feeling produced by the asphelt. It is a green belt around the house which acts as an acoustic and visual barrier.

When there is a wide stretch of land around the house, either forest or garden, placing the swimming pool is straight forward. One can even go so far as designing special surroundings for the pool, choosing the most suitable sizes, materials and plants.

Building up the landscape is the opposite of treating it as a passive object. It implies working on a given area with the aim of influencing the way people perceive it. Whoever constructs a landscape uses the topographic elements available to them, the plant species that grow there, the vistas that can be enjoyed, and plays with all the variables that make up the final effect.

Additionally, working on the landscape implies that a tight project must bear in mind the seasons for the materials and the temperature change. Night has a different ambience to the day. The cyclical passage of time is one of the bases of landscape architecture; the spectator becomes part of the project. Nothing remains the same for long. It is the onlooker who will be the witness of this.

A semi circle part of the pool gently leads the swimmer down some steps into the water.

*A magnificent garden
surrounds the swimming pool
and creates a rich framework
in which to combine sunny,
open spaces with more cosy
and shady recesses and nooks.*

Once we have organized and constructed the garden with zones of varying densities of greenery we can set about approaching the pool and the surrounding forms. The color of the pool water is not an insignificant detail. When the house is near the sea the range of blues has already been introduced into the project. However, on a house plot which has no visual contact with water the predominant tones are green and ochre. It is then that the idea of a blue touch runs through the creator's mind. Or maybe it would be more focused to go for the green hues of the lakes or ponds.

In this pool an intermediate solution has been opted for. The fibre glass covering is white: this makes the water appear a very diaphanous blue. The swimming pool has straight, very strict and precise lines. Symmetry has imposed itself against a background in which ornaments have been kept to a minimum. The motto "less is more", so prevalent in modern architecture, is also present here. This simplicity pays off when the surroundings are beautiful in their own right. The architecture need not compete with nature: everybody comes out winning if the landscape frames the splendour of creation. In some ways it is like an empty stage set on which to play out the choreography of the vacations. One of the main reasons to build the pool on this spot was so that the magnificent views could be enjoyed while basking in the sun, watching the forest softly shimmer as it falls away to the coast.

These aesthetic factors and the ambience created signify that not only is the swimming pool a leisure space in summer but that, moreover, it is an all-year round reference point for all the house.

The form of the swimming
pool is based on a virtual line
that establishes the symmetry.
An abstract element has been
introduced into the landscape.

In the central zone, the terrace
around the pool is cut away
and steps run down into the
bathing area.

Coming through the slender trunks of the pine trees we stumble across a blue haze. It is a swimming pool quite a way off from the house that is reached by going down a small cobbled path through the trees and garden parterres. The zones are divided off by dry stone walls, with the upper part whitewashed. The house is always maintained as a reference point.

A person is linked to their home. It is difficult to know if the house is the form that is most adapted to the environment, our most personal territory in the world, or if it is an extension of ourselves, a second skin. On one hand, all houses are part of the landscape; they are determined by the topography, the orientation and the sunshine. Time and erosion effect the house. However, a house and a garden are simultaneously given life by our activities and movements inside them. Every space acquires meaning when we do something in it, work, rest, eat or play. This is why we can consider it an extension of ourselves. Half way between what we feel as our own and something that does not completely belong to us, a house and a landscape are a form of culture and a language. What a project is like enables us to interpret the tastes, the character and the image of the person who lives there and makes use of it.

In this case what stands out is the purity of the lines, both in the house itself and in the lay out of the garden and the swimming pool. Merely using minimal construction elements and materials, it has been possible to achieve the perfect blending of the artificial parts into the landscape, and at the same time introduce a degree of abstractness into the architectural and natural forms.

The stone walls mark off the different levels and the paths. The whiteness of the lime is a point in common with the house. The rectangular pool has a small side access zone which descends into the water.

The form of the house appears
among the trees presiding
over the garden.

ARCHITECTS AND DESIGNERS:

In the bay, **Rolf Blackstad** (architect).
Unchanged landscape, **Toni Obrador** (designer).
No limits, **André Jacqmain** (architect).
At the foot of the waterfal, **Carmina Claret** (designer).
Blending with the landscape, **Nicolas Desset** (designer).
Constructing a slope, **Toni Obrador** (designer).
On a greek islands, **Xavier Barba** (architect).
Space and proportion, **Rolf Blackstad** (architect).
A moorish pool, **Rolf Blackstad** (architect).
Symmetry and saferty, **Jinty Latimer** (designer).
Classic atmosphere, **Wolf Siegfried Wagner** (architect).
Framing the landscape, **Joan Cardona** (designer).
The reflecting pool, **Toni Obrador** (designer).
Roman tradition, **Georges Scott** (designer).
A pirouette, **Lluis Alonso y Sergi Balaguer** (architects).
A pool with a view, **Lluis Alonso y Sergi Balaguer** (architects);
xyz piscinas (realization); **Fluir** (stair).
Terraces in the patio, **Giovanni Melillo** (architect).
Under the walls, **Toni Vilacasas** (designer).
Between two waters, **Alberto Aguirre** (architect).
A stair case next to the swimming pool, **Norman Cinamond** (architect).
A human landscape, **Renaud Bossert** (architect).
New rural, **Wolf Siegfried Wagner** (architect).
Red house, **Pablo Carvajal** (architect), **Fernando Caruncho** (landscaping).
Between the olives, **Lorenzo Marqués** (architect).
At the frontier, **Lluis Alonso y Sergi Balaguer** (architects);
xyz piscinas (realization); **Fluir** (stair and fountain).
A swimming pool in the garden, **Rosa Clotet y
Joan Llongueras** (architects).
The priviledged secluded hideaway, **Wolf Siegfried Wagner** (architect).
Blue simmetry, **Wolf Siegfried Wagner** (architect).
Light in every corner, **Anick y Jean Ferré** (designers).